It's Not Good, It's Great!

Mary Elizabeth Salzmann

Consulting Editor Monica Marx, M.A./Reading Specialist

Published by SandCastle™, an imprint of ABDO Publishing Company, 4940 Viking Drive, Edina, Minnesota 55435.

Copyright © 2004 by Abdo Consulting Group, Inc. International copyrights reserved in all countries. No part of this book may be reproduced in any form without written permission from the publisher. SandCastle™ is a trademark and logo of ABDO Publishing Company.

Printed in the United States.

Credits
Edited by: Pam Price
Curriculum Coordinator: Nancy Tuminelly
Cover and Interior Design and Production: Mighty Media
Photo Credits: Comstock, Corbis Images, Digital Vision, Eyewire Images, PhotoDisc

Library of Congress Cataloging-in-Publication Data

Salzmann, Mary Elizabeth, 1968-
    It's not good, it's great! / Mary Elizabeth Salzmann.
        p. cm. -- (Sight words)
    Includes index.
    Summary: Uses simple sentences, photographs, and a brief story to introduce six different words: an, good, in, not, put, which.
    ISBN 1-59197-479-8
    1. Readers (Primary) 2. Vocabulary--Juvenile literature. [1. Reading.] I. Title. II. Series.

PE1119.S2342325 2003
428.1--dc21

2003050320

SandCastle™ books are created by a professional team of educators, reading specialists, and content developers around five essential components that include phonemic awareness, phonics, vocabulary, text comprehension, and fluency. All books are written, reviewed, and leveled for guided reading, early intervention reading, and Accelerated Reader® programs and designed for use in shared, guided, and independent reading and writing activities to support a balanced approach to literacy instruction.

Let Us Know

After reading the book, SandCastle would like you to tell us your stories about reading. What is your favorite page? Was there something hard that you needed help with? Share the ups and downs of learning to read. We want to hear from you! To get posted on the ABDO Publishing Company Web site, send us e-mail at:

sandcastle@abdopub.com

SandCastle Level: Beginning

Featured Sight Words

an	good
in	not
put	which

Pete pretends he is an airplane.

Nate's grandpa is a good fisherman.

Betsy helps her grandma in the garden.

Mae is reading the book, not her grandma.

Sal put her hands over her grandpa's eyes.

Jim's grandma knits a sweater, which is blue.

Jon's Grandpa

Jon helps his grandpa put a burger on a bun.

They do not drop it.

They read in the afternoon.

Jon decides which book to read.

They make ice cream.

Jon wants an ice-cream cone.

Jon says, "It's not good, it's great!"

More Sight Words in This Book

a	it
do	make
he	on
her	the
his	they
is	to

All words identified as sight words in this book are from Edward Bernard Fry's "First Hundred Instant Sight Words."

Picture Index

airplane, p. 5

blue, p. 15

burger, p. 16

garden, p. 9

ice-cream cone, p. 20

sweater, p. 15

About SandCastle™

A professional team of educators, reading specialists, and content developers created the SandCastle™ series to support young readers as they develop reading skills and strategies and increase their general knowledge. The SandCastle™ series has four levels that correspond to early literacy development in young children. The levels are provided to help teachers and parents select the appropriate books for young readers.

Emerging Readers
(no flags)

Beginning Readers
(1 flag)

Transitional Readers
(2 flags)

Fluent Readers
(3 flags)

These levels are meant only as a guide. All levels are subject to change.

To see a complete list of SandCastle™ books and other nonfiction titles from ABDO Publishing Company, visit **www.abdopub.com** or contact us at:
4940 Viking Drive, Edina, Minnesota 55435 • 1-800-800-1312 • fax: 1-952-831-1632